Imagine
Morning

Poems of Companionship
& Solitude / Eric Forsbergh

Steve,
Please enjoy, and
your poem is
on page 94.

cheers, Eric

Richer Resources Publications
Arlington, Virginia

Imagine Morning: Poems of Companionship & Solitude
Eric Forsbergh

Richer Resources Publications
1926 N. Woodrow Street
Arlington, Virginia 22207 USA

ISBN 978-1-935238-45-4
LCCN 2013954517

Book design by Sally Zakariya

Published by Richer Resources Publications
Printed in the United States of America

To Yvonne,

my lifelong muse,

still and always, a mystery and delight

Acknowledgements

Prizes

1977 University of Tennessee Knickerbocker Poetry Prize
      for "Sleep in Nagasaki"

2010 Hampton Roads Writers Conference Poetry Prize
      for "The Boat"

2013 Poetry Society of Virginia, Edgar Allen Memorial Prize
      for "Medical Mission, Guatemala, 1997"

2013 Poetry Society of Virginia, Anne Spencer Memorial Prize
      for "The First Dragonfly"

2013 Poetry Society of Virginia, Karma Dean Ogden Memorial
      for "Once the Grunt Decides"

Publications

2013 "Eleanor" and "Four Haiku on the Theme of Falling In Love"
      appeared in But Does It Rhyme (www.butdoesitrhyme.com)

2012 "The Way of Words," "Our Fear of Doctors," "A Story's
      Weight," and "The Ukrainian Pharmacist" appeared in The
      Poet's Domain (Live Wire Press)

CONTENTS

I. COMPANIONSHIP

II. Solitude

I

COMPANIONSHIP

The White Gull

At night, returning home from work,
frayed and late, you and I splash dryly
through the windward leaves piling along the walk
and sidling up against the house: oak, maple, tulip poplar.
Their crinkled backs are bent, and imitating paper claws.
The hump of a single leaf lay by the door below the light,
at second glance, a toad
in plainest brown, festooned with bumps.
He squatted in a perfect pool of light,
waiting for the fall of insects from the hot bulb,
and waited every night through summer.
Why did he become our homely reassurance?

Most days disintegrate like ash
at first grasp of memory, which only stows
the bright and curious, as does the crow.

Remembering that day in Wales, on a cliff,
we braced against a heavy blowing from the Irish Sea.
The crying gulls careened.
Our hair, plastered back, whipped
across our faces when we turned to speak.
Our voices burst apart as they left the hollows of our mouths.
Far below, the surging waves were pounding
into tall and narrow coves, sending towers of spume
to hesitate aloft, and then collapse.
This scene, fixed upon an evanescent hour in a life,
will mix within the mill of memory,
able to transcend, malleable as any other memory,
as long as there is blood to beat.

Yet, what will we do with these other days,
brown, piling by the door?
Our toad waits, secured in place
by every meal of fallen bugs.
Still, the preened white gull of our wishes
has learned to turn a smooth, sharp wing,
soaring up along the slightest columnar drafts,
when all the sea is calm and pewter gray.

ELEANOR

She could pull a hockey stop
before the age of nine,
an airborne girlish glitter off her blades
spraying ice at me.
Our winter snow was surely eight kids deep.
She gripped her stick, a four-boy hand-me-down,
with certainty,
flicking at the puck.
What could I learn from Eleanor,
my torso loose, my face drawn out in fascination?
Someone very different: Girl—I thought—
out on miles of vacant ice edging town,
a chunk of Maine.
My feet splayed. My ankles bent.
I could have done as well in shackles,
not knowing how to skate.
I watched her jump the groaning cracks.
I thought the puck would skitter out of sight.

Yet in that school-day rite of Spring,
when polio might sprinkle around
a share of shriveled limbs,
nurses stood starched upright,
with trays of syringes,
as realization jostled down the fourth grade line.
Stepping up to get the swab and jab, Eleanor passed out,
thunk echoing in the gym.
Hockey crumpled in me when she did.
Darting out of line, I leaned over her,
drawn, even today,
to a softness in the restless freckles
now adrift on her unconscious face,
to the shining corona of her long brown hair
fanned out upon the polished floor.

A WIDOWER

It is the clean heat, the powdery sand,
the hooked spine of a white shell.
This is absolute.
There is the stone blue sky
and the blade of a wave.
There is no flesh on this arrangement.

He walks every day.
In the distance,
he is a thin whip
of bent beach grass.

There is no more coming to bed.
Only going to bed.
There is no more terse reply
or its counterpart:
a rain of goodbye kisses
before walking from the station
out to the wet car.

THE MODELS

The way that models
enter through the eye,
it must be for the speckless gold
of their bodies
their fresh breasts
arranged under aluminum lights,
their teeth with liquid sheen,
their button chins.
Seeing fawn hands
showing inert wares,
am I to bend
like Lysistrata's men?
Give me time to look away.
Where does the photographer
want to pry?
The light is so bright,
the air so thin, so odorless,
desire pales on its shaft.

It is you
I will turn toward,
our imperfections suitable
as objects of affection.
I will turn and fold around you,
touch your face.
We will moisten our lips.

Second Story View

At second story level,
through spring rain's attenuations,
white dogwood blossoms float,
balancing on looping twigs, wet, black.
The proscenium of backyard woods extends,
a watercolor rinse of lime
fronted by spatter of redbuds.

The brow of roof line hedges us within its patter.
Rain's transparent threads alternate with hours of mist.
Repetitive as seasons, we move about the bedroom,
folding our same favorite clothes.

Cooling my brow against the window's glass,
I wish the pane would open like the surface of a lake
and tip me into air to swim a slow fall toward earth
where mud would fold around my feet, work beneath my nails.
I'd feel my fingers plunge against roots, worms, larvae of cicada.
The soil swells, unfurling ginger, fern, trillium.
Spikes of hosta jut, as do the seals of Solomon.
May apples in their rain capes tremble in the flick of drops.
Shoots arise so thick my Wellingtons might crush a few.
I'll feel a trickle down my spine. I'll be damp.
But I know my trowel plows best through earth that's wet.

Four Haiku on the Theme of Falling in Love

"Banging two pans, you
chased a bear?" Such a woman!
I thought, unsettled.

    The windy day whips
    hair across your smile. Your hands
    brush back this disguise.

"Natural woman,"
you said as we watched the stars.
Thank you, Aretha.

    Like a tree with nails,
    I've grown around my partly
    hidden wounds. You too?

What Was Revealed

Cloud shadows pass
across rolling features
of the hills
much like the time
I lightly drew
a trailing gauze of silk
across your face.

I had found you
lounging in undulations,
reclined on a Victorian couch,
deep creases in its upholstery,
velvet as full lips.
Under the gliding veil
you held your gaze,
buttoned loosely in a full expectancy,
eyes half-lidded and obliging.

The subtle play of disguise
began to shift and ride
the sheen of silk.
What was revealed
by your eyes,
the parting of your mouth,
lies waiting like an invitation
to be fulfilled
any time I see scattered clouds
crossing a voluptuous ridge
reclined on the horizon.

1979, AND EVEN NOW

It didn't start with alcohol, as smirking rumors do.
He saw her at a college bus stop,
arrested by her Angela Davis look,
afro like an earthly halo.
It soon became everyone else's business.
He had to meet the two sisters at breakfast, up close,
so they could examine him, blonde and in the light.

Out in town, they were watchful every moment.

Finally, in the faint light of someone's apartment,
the breathing eases. The shoulders slump.
Muscles knotted up at the base of the neck relax.
He lights a candle.
She lays her cigarettes and copper lipstick on the dresser.
They fold into one another like opposite hands.
They accentuate each other,
and in that there is delight,
two skin tones that breathe one into the other
like a man's and a woman's two low voices on a pillow.
They wait quietly for sleep, but like any two that young,
each slipping off to thoughts of home.

Biochemistry Lecture

My friends say I've got it bad.
And so I do.
I was acing this class until last week.
Now, by itself, my pen churns out
a few notes before meandering.
The professor explains oxygen exchange.
His insistent chalk taps
like a flame-tipped bird against a hollow tree.
But I've dropped the reins,
and my senses graze in their traces
under a sky drifting in a slow vortex
around you, who are not even here.

I'd been gone awhile.
Before college, the draft had shipped me out to sea.
I smelled for months like bunker oil,
a perfunctory man, belonging only in a jacket
stitched with lightning bolts.
In fact, time has crawled since high school
as I've waited to be compressed into this moment
from where all teenaged longings get released
like steam from valves.

I now emerge from how many years of anesthesia?
Now that I have fogged the glass,
will it be weeks or months before I see you clearly?
If I can just breathe for two more hours
until I meet up with you walking into embryology.
"Ontogeny recapitulates phylogeny."
That part is clear.
I only want to know
does a longer kiss, laden with a purpose,
recapitulate the first kiss?

Our togetherness is like the clouds,
shapeless, full of light,
formed from moisture in each breath,
and like the clouds,
it doesn't matter that we have no destination.

Storm Along a Beach

There is no walk
like one along a storming beach.
You've lost
the modesty of volume
in your clothes,
plastered by the wind.
Gulls are gone.
A spitting rain laces
at your neck and face.
Try to brace yourself
but you will stagger,
slogging in sand.
Like looming white-haired surf
shouldering its way
onto rocks,
thoughts to share
with your lover
explode against ripping wind.
Even when you yell toward her
wind sucks words
out of your mouth
in all directions
as swallows flee a barn.
She might well
be billowed into the sky
like a loosened dress,
voluptuous in its wild flight.
And you may be found inland,
embedded in a hedge,
spent, blown off your bones.

Huddled in the car again,
both of you are emptied out,
ears in a roar.
And for a fast-closing moment,
you'll see each other,
an outer skin removed,
and with it, feel a tingle,
unsure if it's the subtle sting
of rain and sand.

A Story's Weight

I lean into the weight of your story.
Could I have contained myself any less than you
who met her at the college party,
when she sagged into your arms in the narrow hallway,
her eyes adrift, her mouth unguarded?
Five years later? Now you're confused?
Didn't you walk right into the all-consuming fire of the angel
who placed the live coal against your lips
to sanctify your vow?
Didn't you visit the crippled priest for guidance
the day before the two of you slipped on
the steady gleam of gold meant to quiet the hand?
His scar from Vietnam, his pensive eyes,
all informed you of your coming lies.

The next day, you hurried to say that she was prim in pearls.
Now, you tend your imaginary burn in leisure.
Two scuffling boys yell through their spit,
strewing the kitchen floor with Cheerios,
while you're outside, leaning on the mailbox,
staring down a street that bends away like a river.

The Way of Words

When air begins to grow an edge,
animals pursue the sinking arc of sun.
Was it so impossible that I would find
indoors, a rattlesnake up on the windowsill
by the handrail at the landing of the stairs
where late sun's long stroke warms the wood,
and where we pass up to our bed?
You lay napping, the door ajar.

Returning with a shovel,
I approached it quietly, and drew myself up,
arms above my head, torso twisted, tense,
poised in the all-or-none moment,
Greek statuary in a T-shirt.
Drinking in that familiar blunted triangle
set with lashless obsidian eyes,
I sensed my pupils widening
before I rammed the edge in behind its head.
Rattles hissed as it writhed in curls,
falling at my dancing feet
before three frenzied blows distorted
its head into pink pulp,
displaying mangled rows of curved white needles.
You never woke.

After all these years, all our conversations,
all I've had to tell you, sometimes owning up,
my head hung like a blowing horse,
my sentences smeared with the mucus of remorse,
and yet at other times, side-winding over drinks,
circumnavigating in a slow undulation of words
like the ripple of scales,
I've never mentioned this for fear
I'd underestimated you and not the snake.

THE BOAT

A small boat works its way,
a couple aboard, young,
under a florid lake sunset.
Even from a distance they seem new to each other,
their faces within a breath's reach,
their shoulders forward deferentially.
Her slim arms are by her sides.
It's the eyes that carry all communication now.
Being in the confines of this boat, looks that fall away
must return to redirect the mouth's intent.
The motor burbles onward,
making slight headway under a vast sky.
With the sun behind, they are a mere outline
on an unsteady plane of mercury.

What is there in the flight of a single day?
There are no cogent messages
in the reddened half-illumination of their faces.
It is moisture and the play of light
in this blue that overlays the salmon,
peach, mango, running into streaks of pulp
from a blood orange seeming close at hand.

The last red lip of light hugs
the fur-like hills, all in utter silence.
Leaning closer in the darkening boat,
hope picks its way among the words,
shifting weight from foot to foot,
not knowing which to ask:
"Are you to be my brilliant vapor of a dream?"
Or "Will this moment fade to black?"

THE TICK

My wife said,
"I feel something on my back.
Can you look at it?"
A silver-black seed pearl
engorged with her blood, its head dug in
and just below her shoulder blade,
the welt already tight.

I paused,
even after her insistent permission
overran a promise of pain.

Our best household scissors are surgical,
one beak with fine serrations
to keep flesh from slipping off.
She bent forward under the sink light,
head in hands,
fingers spilling through with hair.
One penetrating cut gave up a flap of skin.
At second cut
she arched her back,
an echo of expression
from her lexicon of pleasure,
but inhaled a gasp raked through teeth.
A ruby bead welled up
between stainless beaks.
I pressed for a deeper cut.
Lifting away the tick
I traced by chance a wet red comma
before the chilly burn of alcohol.

In the baggie, its hair-like legs in motion,
the tick would not release
its smear of flesh.

Our secluded conversations,
our rumpled nest of a bed,
our sharing of a peach, fingers wet,
our small admissions,
all are proven to be tighter by this wedge:
a repulsive intimacy,
even one so tiny and succinct.

Physics and Philosophy

My father used to drift among the spheres,
as I, a child, scooted,
scraped my toys along our wooden floors.
Atomic postulates might vie with French quatrains
as he'd be gazing through a second-story wall
at something levitating in the elements.
I wondered where he was.
I thought it could be a room, quite visible to him,
vibrating in the apple tree out back
beyond the shingled simple planes of our house.
At his hobbied carpentry,
his sawdust-sprinkled hands would move about,
slow and purposeful as lobsters.
Even then, even holding an edge,
they could not conjoin his eye's beam,
nor conjugate his thought.

Years later, wearing the likeness of an adult,
I swam into a river
swollen from torrential churn
if only to rub and jar against debris,
granulations of the palpable world:
tractors mired in mud
strings of barbed wire
grease from heaps of plates
rifle reassembly by blindfold
smell of salt in dawn sea
diving into Penobscot Bay
scritch of pencils in a test
incisions in a fetal pig
chilly basins full of autopsy
heat from an abscess needing to be drained
a biopsy I'll excise this afternoon.

Still I hear a non-stop rhetoric
at any street corner I approach:
Confucius tangling with Paine
Einstein head to head with Bohr
Shakespeare at it with Li Po.
And all the while,
inhabiting my gait,
inhabiting the focus furrow in my face
my father drifts along with me.

THE CANOE

At night, along a narrow northern lake
we took our paddles to canoe into
utter silent inky calm.
The full moon, ripe to burst, was hanging low
and just above the water's blackened pane
of glass, and magnified by atmosphere.
Its mottled, white complexion looked sickly
for all its dominance, and we, our eyes
adjusted to dark, bathed in stark cool light,
our features clear as conversation in
the quiet dome, where all the fainter stars
were blocked from view, all minor thoughts submersed,
and though I do not like a trance, I fell.

Your slightest breathing now I've finally learned
to recognize in quiet this profound.
This liquid mirror, black, and miles long,
can carry the coyote's cry from anywhere.
The forest hangs in wait on either shore.
Our fingers intertwined, what years it took
to drop the feeling of a choking vine.
The gleaming paddle lay across my lap.
Its blade allowed another drop to fall.
Beneath the ash of moon, we've now looked past
estrangement found in shadowed eyes and mouth,
and we can be at rest on unknown depths.

THE DAY THE GYM STOOD STILL

My wife's laugh prowled, submerged inside her throat
as she lowered herself slowly, limbs akimbo,
nine months round, into the car.
"Did I think I'd slip unseen into the indoor pool?
I wanted pressure off my spine for just a while.
But once inside, guess what?
The women's locker room, with all those hard bodies."

I imagined sleek and tawny hunters,
after all their repetitions on the Roman chair,
doing up their hair and nails,
oiling down their tans.

"So I simply stripped."

She told how all the chatty air went blank.
Hair dryers clicked and flagellating hair fell limp.
Those who stared would only do it in a mirror.
I imagined motion-acclimated athletic bodies standing stock still,
their minds like herds of horses galloping, galloping far ahead,
galloping forward to some point
beyond the curvature of a gold ring
to the distention of mother earth.

That night, we spooned around that awkward,
grand and naked fullness,
its out-front weight,
its brief swell of a moving foot,
propelling us forward, forward.
And all the while,
mechanical like most men,
reductive by analogy,
I held aloft the one brass ring.

POEM ON BEHALF OF A FRIEND

What you have so far will work its day.
You've asked and I'll assist,
my finest friend.
You'll want to honor her,
watch the weightless nature
of delight as it sweeps her face.
We won't try trochees, dactyls.
Any pothole can break her mood.
Let's not use onomatopoeia.
She's not a purring cat.
Align your iambs to a rhythm
like the constancy of waves.
Consonance and assonance
will warm her sensibility
like two massaging hands.

Try extended metaphor.
She breathes a life
into her wooden violin.
Yet stiff, high-strung,
inattentive most of the day,
it never seeks her company,
only the reverse.
It remains a demanding lover,
often out of tune with her,
with its arrogant long neck,
its vanity of lacquered curls,
and never satisfied
except by her most subtle touch.
But you? You stand before her,
the warm blood companion
offering a supple kiss
to wield music by.

I'll crouch in the dark bushes
like a Cyrano.
I'll spool out your lines
so only you will hear. Go now.
Enunciate them up to her.
Surprise her lounging heart
as she leans on her casement
fingering the night air.

By All Rights

By all rights, shouldn't more of us have died by now?

On a whim, at night, on unfamiliar roads,
my teenage sister walked on top of a narrow stone wall,
not knowing, even though she felt cool air
rising up one flank, the rail bed was sixty feet below.

Do Providence and Luck divide the work?
Providence, the trinity of time within a single eye,
directs her hand as light and calm as silk.
And Luck, the dumbest kind, arrives early, late, sometimes never,
feels around in his pocket for dispensations, and flings them out,
sometimes pelting the wrong recipient.
His knobby forehead glistens as he says, " I just ran out."

As I boarded the plane
to see my sister in Lexington,
did I happen to see you, Luck?
Will you wager on that stud?
I shuffled with my dreary carry-on,
my personal effects already pawed as if by some coroner
fastidious in blue rubber gloves.
I headed toward the back of the can,
through First Class.
It was you after all: heavy, shirt two buttons open,
gold rope languorously reclined in sweaty hair.
Untouchable, you mopped your face while paying for a drink,
your wallet as fat as a tick.
Are you verging on a heart attack?
Is it that you fear to fly? You should see yourself.

Providence, laconic in her speech, walks ceaselessly,
the imprimatur of scripture in her bearing.

Among barns in Tennessee, as children,
sister and I watched the horse trainers breaking in the yearlings.
Kicking dust, the roans and whites would whip their heads,
trying, failing to break the ropes,
careening into the planks of the corral.
Silent, I studied the trainers for their reactions.
I noticed they loved to wear
the horseshoe ring with seven diamond chips.
Cautious, yet they all took pains to go to church.

TO A YOUNG ISLAMIC PROFESSOR

This she told me
after several years.
Since I am wholly different,
I see it with my pocket lens.
I keep it like a testament.

She arranges her hijab
before she leaves the modest house.
But first, like scriptures on a bathroom mirror,
she enumerates her list of why.

To admire her husband
as she herself becomes admired.
Her eyes flow over his body
like warm rain over rocks.

To sound a note
from her lectern at university,
a sharp note to pierce the vacuum bell
of those texting for a date,
sprawled as if they're still in bed.
To warn that,
every day, in convulsing nations,
famished youth spill from every alley
like ants out of a burning log
to swarm the cordoned palace square.
"That extra seat on which
you've draped your legs?
Even stripped for a beating,
they want that seat."

To unveil her heart, to link into the fight.
Alone, ablutions flown to Allah,
she'd tasted every minute of her hour in line to vote
as squares of sunlight crept, aligned,
across the polling station's floor.
The night before, she'd vaulted out of bed,
jerked the window latch to gasp at Boston's air,
sarin imminent in her dream mouth,
vision double in her splintered doorway in Aleppo.

CLAMMING IN GREAT BAY

In sweeps of coves along Great Bay, where salt
and fresh surge daily back and forth, my dad,
brother and I would take a break at noon
from hours on the tractor mowing hay,
or moving rocks, or cutting up the last
year's snow-split fallen limbs: to oyster, clam,
maybe hook a lamprey eel, slick black tail
curling in mid-air, its mouth a dark pit,
serrated rings akin to Dante's view.
The silky mud for clamming, inky, soft
as coastal fog, was dotted with the pin
holes of our feast. Our rubber boots would slurp
among the squirts, and breaching glossy muck
with rakes, we'd harvest there an evening's meal.
The oysters were a guess, often near rocks.
We'd rinse and pry, and once the gristle's cut,
we'd play them in the mouth, then swallow fast.
Immersed in dog-dead work again, we took
more sustenance from sun and clouds at play
on fields, meandered banks of tidal grass,
grizzled shagbarks, a flight of crisp white swans.
At times, a wind would race across the bay,
raise feathered spume, before it burst uphill
to carry through the bow-bent hissing trees.

How few remain of these salt water farms.
Conservancies and builders hammer back
and forth, and I am of two Senecas.
As Roman Seneca, imperial
intents have poured the concrete of my barn,
then paved my asphalt road, then piled in
aluminum for one more floating dock.
As Seneca the tribe, who traded with
the Abenaki, lately I've begun
to trade away my vanity. Baled hay
beneath the sun is now my airy sweat
lodge. Hawks return. But still, the Senecas
tread back and forth, while I, asleep in grass,
dream of salt air, the clouds, the honk of geese.

SKIFF

A skiff.
Two lobsters.
A few gulls float
the drift of tide.
We'll lounge together,
on the island sand. Pulling
oars is calm, with all its repetition. Haul
the skiff up in the breakers
in back of the island. We'll form
a visual break using the skiff, backed
up on sand. The rocky island is discrete,
few in features. Two lobster boats
chug, off the beach, and cut their engines,
rocking on a lounging tide, behind
the island. Gulls wheel in closer.
Tides cut sandy moats around beach boulders.
After lobster, we'll nap
back behind the pea-pod skiff,
with two boats hauling traps close off-shore.
Cut gurry and the gulls descend.
You can hear a pulley wheel squeak
across the calm tide.
Off the sides of two boats,
gurry baited lobster traps thrown back
will break the glassy drift of tide.

CASTLE ISLAND FISHING CAMP, MAINE

Two fishermen, flannel plaid, tackle boxes, poles,
shamble down to their aluminum boat,
its nose up in the sand
like a drunk laid in gently for the night by friends.
Skidding across blue miles of lake,
morning sunlight glares against each squinting face.
Their talk resembles bait, in bits and cuts:
beer, Papi's homer, wives, sandwiches.
Yet lurking, surging, about to hit the surface
through their drowsiness,
obsessed anticipation—a tingle
like amphetamine, fully hooked—
plunges into a tangled filament
of spinners, poppers, jigs, spoons,
luggers, boogers, treble-hooks and fry.
Count in weather. Count in bugs.
Count in shade and shafts of sun,
and how those angle beneath the water.
Count in sunken logs, boulders.
Finally, distorted by the wobble of green glass,
count in the maddening simplicity of fish,
pectoral fins forever sculling,

Six Haiku on the Theme of Marriage

Hugely pregnant, you
split baby's pool: upended
turtle on wet grass.

> The moon's tangled in
> trees, your hair and hands. It smooths
> your curving bare back.

Tree roots grow into
a boulder's seam. Like this, you
crack my stubbornness.

> Fat, round faces in
> a frame, we wish now for their
> runny-nose kisses.

In other women's
smiles, temptation shifts like blown
sand. I need firm ground.

> "Love the bride of your
> youth." Psalms. You wear the toil of
> years, and so do I.

Marriage When It's Tough

Sitting motionless
is it the same
to watch the rain distort the view
through sagging windowpanes
as to watch a fire flicker,
consume its log,
becoming ash
as smoke writhes up?
Your hands hang limp.
The thought of food sickens you.
Your eyes drift,
too tired to swim.
Now no longer in the present tense,
blinkered,
you and she can only see ahead in parallel
as friends attempt to say
"Look, we see the lines converge."
They cannot.
Perspective itself
will bend what's straight.

You tamp down turbulent intents.
Go ahead.
Try it.
Hold your head up with dignity
while you stoop to sweep the shards
of that innocent dish you threw down
like some gauntlet
of self-ridicule
against the kitchen floor.
You are waterlogged and burning all at once.

A Wife Absorbed

We like to keep each other company,
occasionally with dialogue.
There are no undertows.

While you cook,
you brush across my view
as I set the table,
the careful angle
of each plate, napkin, glass, spoon,
like a theatre set
an audience of two appreciates.
A proscenium of bottled wine awaits.
I become reflected
in that radiant happiness of yours
arising from the spoons and spatulas.
A measure of olive oil into the hot pan
makes a startled sound.
Disordered vegetables,
throwing color everywhere,
get magnified by bright pot curves.

I like to hang around
when you turn dirt for planting bulbs.
Call me if you need the narrow trowel.
A wisp of hair keeps falling in your eyes
like a song stuck in your head.
You bear fresh scratches
as a jeweler displays her bracelets
for a customer,
angled across the forearm,
red threads strung with garnet dots.

I drink coffee, idling out of gear.
Sitting on the couch, your knees drawn up,
you cannonball into your book.
By your eye's intent,
your mind pulses along the story line
like an otter surging
after a glimmering fish.

A Touch's Length

When we're within a touch's length
it doesn't matter what we do.
Was it you or I who said it first?
The spin of earth
lends its burly weight
behind which every clock hand
orbits on its spline,
interlocking us with motions in a day.
Tree rings make a record of our years,
narrow in our drier times,
wider when we flowed
with mutual nutrition.

Pillowed in the dark,
you pose your hand
along my neck to slow
my pulse within its banks
as I begin to drift.

I know when you're asleep—
your breathing slows,
a dreamless pace at first.
I've known it since before our children
showed their quizzical faces
at our bed's edge.
I know it still, grown and gone.

As we lie, limbs disarranged,
I've turned your warm palm
to my cheek.
I grasp it as if to stop
that clock hand from its rounds.
And yet, where darkness heightens hearing,
there persists a ticking from the far end of the hall.

A Wet Snow

How could I be wedged inside this winter house,
locked into my spousal pantomime
when you are simply reading in another room?
A walk may smooth the joints.
Towering black skeletons, outlined in wet snow,
waft their fingers, intricate as filigree.
Some limbs, split by heavy snow,
expose the flow of grain,
calm, then splintered in a twist, then calm again.
The sky's gray quilt suffocates the time of day.
I walk the lush cuts of
a pillowed landscape,
where sound gets suffocated just as well.
The middle ground is not enough to bear my weight.
At the bend, the river's surface
carries a glossy twist like drowned black hair.
Along its bank, thin ice inscribes its silver hooks.

From nowhere, a cardinal flashes,
a sudden red cut.
My hands uncramp.
My face resumes its normal beat of blood.

That Look of Yours

That swirl of small fry
twisting at the surface of the lake?
It's like that look of yours
working its way across your face
from some new pulse of thought:
a fish with weight
roiling minnows from below.
A smile—if it is one—crimps corners
of your mouth. But you won't speak.
If that's your fish, will it feed on silence?
Will it swim among the weeds,
among shadows from the leaning trees?
A few can swim for years
through subtleties of shade,
continuing to grow as certain fish will do
as they disturb the water time to time,
inaccessible and silent as the moon.

I'm not made of hooks.
I won't cast one at you.
I slapped a deerfly off my neck,
a question buzzing around my head
I've finally caught.
I'll toss it out
where it will lie on top, a lure,
a dimple on the water
bending the surface tension.
I only ask a fleeting look:
its twist of muscle at the surface break,
its slippery shimmer,
its glimmer in a gradient of hues.
Just as a Northern Pike consumes anything alive,
it's the species of the fish that worries me.

Diane

My sister's wife
strides each dawn the outer fence of their Tennessee farm.
She hitches along in a rolling gait,
and slings her hand out for a shake.
They cut each other's hair with a tobacco knife,
it seems, and almost to the roots.
She tends to swallow back her voice,
even for tender wishes,
her words in an accent
that tracks her to the county of her birth.
She'll not care to imitate my urban politesse,
my cautious tinting of each unctuous phrase.
Her comments and remarks taste like pure spring water,
with mineral tang, out of a mountain cleft.
In church, she cradles her mother's venous spindly hand.

She stows a gun inside the glove box of her truck.
Under their bed, two more wait, loaded and immaculate.
A folding knife hugs her hip,
because death, in its asymmetric hatchet face,
glowering among dark tree trunks
just beyond the porch's pool of light
often has befallen those who won't disguise themselves.

When springtime sun glimmers up from scattered straw,
each end of their hillside barn gets opened, allowing it to breathe.
In its tack room hang skins of animals she tanned.
Like the frozen motion of a figure skate
balanced on its toe pick,
her cleaver juts up from its butcher's block.

And when I leave for home, she bakes up her fondness
as an old-fashioned coconut cake to take along.
Gripping each other's backs, kissing each other's faces,
we pour ourselves as milk into this moment,
unpasteurized.

Meditation on a Portrait

In this portrait, now hanging in my living room,
tension pulses still between the painter and the posed.
Her nose and cheeks are slightly red.
Her hand clutches a white kerchief,
Her long fingers are closed, knuckles on her hips.
Fixed on the artist, her dilated eyes are luminous.
Beneath the short dense ruby
brushstrokes of full lips,
her chin is tense.
He's painted her as if her beauty
were their battleground.

Her velvet robe is mostly open,
the same robe my mother played in as a child,
dragging about the heavy hem of pretend.
He—my grandfather, young, a Dutch classicist,
emboldened by the utter instinct of his brush—
pretended to need another sitting,
when he could wield her expertly with cupped hands around her waist
when the house was empty, but for them,
when the studio window's light cascaded through parted curtains
spilling to the floor, across to the plush, Persian red Victorian couch.
Then he could seduce her with her own face
between cigarettes.
Life is short, art is long, they always said.
Two on a match.

Now here I stand before his portrait of her.
Her face and open neck invite me,
her lips voluptuous and cold.
The pulse arising in the hollow of her throat
has been a hardened grease for eighty years.

Up close, escaped from a brush, lies
the single bristle of a hog embedded in the paint.
Did she stand before him and tease that brush,
fresh and pliable, across the landscape of her skin?
Did she purse out smoke, and draw it up her nostrils,
as if to advertise her talents, so he'd be aching for the sight of her?
How it looks so like a moving snake.

They flew like birds before a forest fire.
And it all came true. Before old age
could desiccate their hair and skin,
they were gone upon the flicker of a match.

The Middle Managers

It's Wednesday coffee, early.
On a café table
balance two cardboard cups full of black.
Did we fashion this life?
Could we have mustered more?
Fine lines have been crossed and re-crossed.
We see them netted on each other's face.
We've drained the decades off
into an endless sponge,
strained against the wheel of work,
taken the golden goad right between the ribs.

But here and now,
coffee's odor permeates every narrow crease
and each of us has hung up
his abraded carapace.
Here, at dawn, the air smells empty and quiet.
We thumb down lumps.
We lumber on in ill-fit shoes.

But balanced now, bright in this moment,
our parting handshake braces us
before our vertigo returns,
before the needles of a self-inflicted anesthesia
turn upon themselves, becoming hooks.

Alzheimer's Wing

On a late afternoon,
we visited my wife's mother, eighty-eight.
I imagine her seeing through a kaleidoscope
at vivid fragments, shaken loose,
tumbling with every turn.
Or as a two-year-old who sees
the great round sun-struck window
from deep inside the darkened nave at Reims.
Between questions we might put to children,
we looked past her in silence
when we noticed the husband of room 37
doddering along, slow as nightfall.
He shuffles down from the independent wing, they say.
They say he stays past midnight,
lying in bed with his wife.
Does he gently bend her wrist, her elbow too,
like the slow retraction of a swan's neck
to slide it down the armhole of her gown?
Does he lay his hand,
like a nesting wren with opened wings,
between her shoulder blades?
Does he purse his dry lips against her dry neck,
where she might remember him
without the veil of words?
Perhaps, today,
she thinks she's tuckered out,
bare feet scuffed
from playing in the yard on swings.

In a Potter's Field

My grandfather lies somewhere, I was told,
in the potter's field.
A lawn unmarked, mowed to velvet,
a low sward of grass like a ship bottom
where the ballast of community was packed—
handymen, chimneysweeps, porters,
a clutch of artists and the ilk,
all beneath arthritic oaks
of New England coast.
Rockport's cemetery map
has this section penciled in as rectangles:
boxes tacked closed, each with its skeleton,
each wedged in like parquet floor.
Upon whom do I walk?
Light plays with leaves like rippled water
across this lush swale where indigent lie.
They came to rest,
limp and transparent as pooled rain
soaking into soil, having trickled down
among the hillside's upright stones
that were paid in full,
erected on the crest
to get a view of the sea,
including the plot
my mother chose so carefully.

II

Solitude

The Solitude Of Memory

Do you remember that man, newly dead?
The one at dawn, across the yellow stripe,
sliced into the highway
through the heart of Guatemala?
His limbs gawked
up from the pavement awkwardly
as if he'd tumbled from Jacob's ladder
clambering to dodge the goons.
His clothes were barely scuffed.
His face was freshly shaved.
Not a teardrop of blood.

You can't remember him.
You were concerned elsewhere
on a morning offering its normal void.
He occupies my retinas
like a flashbulb imprint,
faded, yes, but permanent.

Mulling through a lunch in Richmond,
I watch your jaw at work.
The fresh rolls seem inviting,
but vinegar filters back a dark red light
from the cruet in its cage.

That dawn, I wondered
if his hand might move.
It never does.
Not at lunch.
Not when I squeeze my eyes shut
as I soap down in the shower.

When I watch your clothing
start to separate on fingertips
as we undress for each other,
he gets deposited in his mortal posture
outside on the hallway floor.
But not for long
will he permit the stay.

A Forward Sway

An inchworm instructed me.
A month among Buddhist monks
might not.
Perhaps it is a penchant
for the visual.

On a picnic whim
I lay in maple shade
among remains of lunch:
rind of cheese, mango peel,
a disassembled afternoon
soaked in lassitude,
on lush grass.
I floated into half-sleep.
Sounds grew intimate yet far.
After intermittent time,
I opened one eye,
my easy eye,
noticing an inchworm
on my close-curled arm:
its reach, its touch,
its hind release, its flexing fold.
Its repetition.
Six tendril feet in front.
Four tendril feet in back.
Nothing in between.
An umlaut standing on its dots.
Arriving at my fingertip
it swung its head to search,
rear feet bearing up an inch's weight
before it circled over and around.

The misery i've harbored,
its mockery, its aftermath,
by not recalling this:
Sway forward,
stretch and touch,
let go what's behind.

Great Depression Portraiture

It was grim earnings.
I could tell by the way
my mother described food:
clam broth, bread, lobster bodies
—no tail or claws.
The little girl always remembered
no sugar in the house.

With each portrait unveiling,
her father wrapped his European dignity
and his hands,
stained from paint and cigarettes,
around a twisted cloth,
stifling a cough.
He surged to capture inner flame
like a moth that beats
on summer evening windowpanes
where colored imprints
of the dust from wings remains.
The candle spits, emits a curl of smoke.

Eighty years along,
amid their bequests,
portrait sitters, each in a favored posture
flatly survey the gloom of dining rooms.
At rest, the servants' swinging door
admits a blade of light
from the kitchen
where three next generations
laugh around the laden board.

Instantaneous Insensibility

Instantaneous insensibility:
a term laced on like rubberized boots
by cattlemen at the slaughterhouse,
meaning sudden death.
No albino crow perches in the rafters,
hopping down to stretch one wing
as if to point the way.
Day on day, one by one,
blood overwhelms
each collapsed brain.

Am I the one to mouth
my cousin's final prayers?
She died obliterated,
2 AM, drunk.
The captain of the fire truck
descending from his elevated seat,
emerged through the darkness
in iridescent yellow stripes.
Not yet seeing into the flame-lit ditch,
he first came across her shoe,
upright,
poised to walk the white line.

MEDITATION ON APPALACHIA

Among the countless hollowed slopes of Appalachia,
the many tail-ends of valleys wending out
from Knoxville, narrowing eventually
to paths that vanish into curtained leaves,
where, once inside, only dots of sunlight
are permitted to speck the forest floor,
or creep across the mounds of moss, as slow
and imperceptible as deer whose breath
is stilled upon the snapping of a branch,
the shiny beetle crawls unhurriedly
to find the pulpy log's decay.

THELMA

We thought to check on her, the farm agent and I,
driving out to see an air-conditioned tractor.
Back in March, the blanched countryside around us,
she'd put her bucket down to squint, before we turned to leave.
Now, we snake our way up the switchbacks into her valley.
Gravel on the hardpan road pops beneath our tires.
An abandoned twelve-pew church leans
into a couch of pokeweed, berries bright purple as the robe.
Trailers are suspended on weedy cinder blocks,
ready to cast off, ready to ride the second Flood.
An outstretched hawk wheels above.

She's been rooted in her cabin eighty years, thirty five alone.
What could we pretend to know of solitude,
our wallets packed with children's photographs?
We stride the last few washouts. The rusted roof emerges,
logs settled like fallen ribs.
Pear trees, in dense black tangles, lean beside the flattened gate.
We pick our steps among the brown fruit sweetening the grass.
Surprised that we are fully flesh, she steps out on the porch.
Morning shadows rake the clumpy yard.
She stops before us, at a distance.
Her eyes and fingers dart about, composing our presence.
Her skin is fibrous, pulled-back hair the color of soured milk.
We view the valley opening below, to houses, barns
built, bought, sold, rebuilt, sold again.
"People don't hardly know what they want no more."
The agent offers her the sparse mail of a month.

She walks the cycle of daily chores,
grassy footpaths laid a century ago.
Does her imagination drift as she stoops at the mossy spring?
Is it like those crayfish, jelly-white as cataracts,
fingering their way across the sightless pools
of valley caves? When she carries wood through fog among the trees,
where beds of bluebells drip silently, is all half-seen?

Are the hours meted out to prayer?
Do supplications rise upon the drafts of air?
Beyond the ridge, the domes of clouds appear
as a city arrayed in gleaming white.

Back at the truck, we pick our boot soles clean
with screwdrivers, and lean into the cab
to check the implacable clock in the dash.
The seasons, the tractor's throttle, the rhythm of the baler,
the children's growth marks on the kitchen door frame,
the phrasing of a prayer,
all will serve to rein my pace.
The everlasting hawk twitches its wings,
spirals upward on the warmth of day.

Carrion

A great fish slumps, dead
beside the road. In fact,
an abandoned greenhouse,
its thin white bones of sagged aluminum,
its countless panes like scales
falling inward piece by shining piece.
Fabric tatters hang like desiccated skin.
The weeds rebury it.

Initially, the entryways
get broken down, left hung askew.

Seagulls when they scavenge
have a habit.
They first pick out the eyes.

You, Imagining The Sky

You're a lucky one
living where the weather counts.
Mares' tails whisk the sky of haze.
Every neighbor up and down the road
sees what's coming,
one eye bred for atmosphere.
A few sleeves of rain are soon perceived
far to the counties south.
When clouds gather to a slurry
in late day muggy air
to spill a thrashing rain,
you'd better make a run for the barn,
boots clomping up the slope.
Your yellow oilskin trails
like a flapping fish's tail,
as the leading sheet of rain begins
to mill away the hill behind you.

You can smell the musk
along the darkened stalls.
A horse's patient eye
might be the only gleam
until your own adjust.
The tin roof rattles as loudly
as if nails poured down from the afterlife.
Streams of water sluice
down every seam.

Imagine morning,
crisp as hay and cool.
Imagine every hoof print
brimmed with rain,
like back up mirrors
spangled across a barnyard lot,
sparkling in mud.
Imagine morning fanning out
its brightly polished blades
among the trees.

Do We Become Our Parents?

At first, he seems like John Brown,
instead of my itinerant great-grandfather
bent upon abolishing all sin, not one.
I'm examining a brittle photograph
lightly in my fingers,
yet it carries weight like something
issued from a furnace in Leviticus.

The two of them stand full against the sun.
His long beard juts, angled like a shovel blade.
His eyes fixate on far
but along their path
they bore a hole
right through the camera,
right through the photographer and me.
His mouth is set like a sprung trap,
clamped down to pulverize the demon's wrath.
My great-grandmother
stands like an appendage
in a white bonnet made snug.

Horseback in Michigan in 1903,
halting at any bare board church,
did he startle Dutch parishioners?
Perhaps a few supposed
that what begins as Swedish dialect
could fly apart to speech in tongues.

Should I wonder then
at my grandfather?
He stood trim in uniform,
an artillery officer, an engineer.
I knew him as a silky raconteur,
a man who'd kiss a woman's hand
with full intent.
Even in a public place,
he'd weave a secluded nest
around that evanescent moment
of the lips, the touch of fingertips,
shuttling between his academic English
and his lustrous French.

Chain Gang

The chain gang shambled
up ahead.
I felt the car begin to slow.

Alligator alley
sawing sound of bugs
heat seething off the road

and my uncle Jim,
a gruff love,
profane Navy talk
a boy of eight
could not forget.
Jesus H. Christ
accompanied us everywhere.

The car slowed more.
Leaning on hot metal
of the rolled down
back-seat window frame,
I saw shackles, shovels,
stripes. To me,
their faces could have been
crumpled cans,
as if they'd lost their heads
sometime past.

In his hand, he hid
a pack of cigarettes
like the palming of a coin.
And when the shotgun sheriff turned,
Jim flipped it to the manacled feet
of the closest man.

Did I see black, or white,
or Seminole?
I don't recall.
I saw eyes, trapped,
broiled red.
I saw mouths gape open
for a chance to breathe.

Flying into Portland

In glint of sun
the sea looks like chain mail,
a swath of silvery steel, mutable,
in motion from what underlies.

Crossing that white-feathered hem of surf
stitched between sea and land
the plane banks hard.
An odd comfort,
compressed from underneath, into my seat,
compressed from front to back
with eighty-five or so:
a boyhood carnival Tilt-A-Whirl
dropping me again into a New England youth.

From a thousand feet,
Portland Head lighthouse
stands like a stump,
foreshortened from above,
its shadow undulating
long across the rocks.

Lower, inland, across neighborhoods perched
on black sticks fanned out in late afternoon,
shafts of sunlight intersperse
as if to cut beneath the landscape,
peel up the artifice of lawns,
reveal to each adult
notions of a shallow past
out of rocky soil.
Enlarging cul-de-sacs
slip by quickly in the stream.
Only ballfields and churches
clarify themselves.
I remember playing ball.

I remember singing
in a children's choir,
singing upward
through an unblemished ceiling
into what I was convinced
was a clear sky
populated by a host,
observant from above.

Columbus Day

The lake has lost its lush appeal.
Your hands don't yet clutch a coffee cup,
or tug down a knitted cap for frost.
Luminous the yellow leaves,
voluminous the canopy
before its drifting swirl begins,
triggered by a snap of atmosphere.
The sun begins to belly low,
its halo crossing each back-lit leaf
like a stepping stone.
Torn-cloth caws of crows arise,
black darts piercing a yellow field.
Green strokes of branches have vanished,
revealing summer's predatory haunts.
All is lit in sunflower, down to the stony ground,
edging the brittle sheen of lake expanse.
Far overhead, a silent jet
inscribes a straight line south,
contrail like a pipe cleaner.
Their moisture lost, leaves shrink and curl.
Opening gaps and separating seams,
the whole begins to pull apart,
a landscape laid exposed for silent snow.

Blueberry Picking

I wake beside you, at the cabin,
in blue-black aura of dawn, hungry,
gnawing gristle of a departing dream.
Maundering thoughts stir like warming snakes.
Silent as abandonment, I leave,
go down among damp rocks,
and slide the canoe into the lake
to find the fatness of blueberries along the far shore.
I stroke my gleaming paddle once into the glass,
and lifting it as I glide outward, wait:
for breath to find purchase in my lungs,
for ripples to recede in rings,
for an osprey's outline to stretch its wings,
for looming shapes to coalesce as trees,
for dawn's pallor to flush out into
uncontested colors of day,
for restlessness to cease its nipping
underneath my skin
like fish that hit the surface from below.
Sky in violet bathes the ribs of the canoe.

I paddle through mist's feathered landscape,
until the far bank, hugged in moss, protrudes.
Leaning over water, bushes hang thick with berries:
green, purple, blue, blue in clusters,
a size of blue like some bird's eyes,
I guide the canoe underneath
and with a pawing eagerness start pulling bunches.
They patter onto the canoe bottom,
bouncing everywhere, a feast for bears and saints alike,
tart enough to cut the cloying from their sweetness,
rebalancing my gratitude, making it replete.

March Snow

Weak and late it arrives.
Barely frozen,
its huddled flakes
fall lumpen
out of fat damp air.
These don't fly like January's flakes.
Tiny, swift as ballerinas,
they swirled so thick
in columned drafts
the neighbor's house
seemed to be in motion too,
restrained from lifting off its cellar
weighted down with roots and coal.

Under this last storm, incipient of spring,
bare trees still clack their black branches
at its intermittent gusts.
Curled under earth,
April prods her greening fingers
among rocks and roots,
through slush,
up. Her summer sisters wait to join.

Portland's harbor under stretch of tides
nudges floes of ice.
Streets display their wet skins
like sleeping seals.
Each bush sags, laden with a snow cap
that cracks open like an egg.

No one buys a shovel now.
Boil a cup of tea and sit.

MEDITATION ON SUNSET

Onto the surface of the lake, the late sun throws
a brilliant path of beaten copper,
and with each breeze, it flickers apart,
assuming the scales of an iridescent snake
always shimmering toward me.
At my feet, dark water is its mouth.
I am transfixed, flecks of light embedding
deep into the orbits of my eyes.
I may avert my gaze, as infants do,
or wait, just wait,
for mute and soothing stars.

Mt. Katahdin

I've taken up a purpose to be small.
My snowshoes crump deep powder.
Columnar hemlock, spruce and pine
surround pillowed domes
of snow's massive silence.
Light attenuates
beneath each buckled branch.
Dead trees tilt askew,
visual cacophony
weighted on the living's limbs,
a hung tension.
I ascend alone
among house-sized boulders
broken from a batholith
cleaved by ice.
I clamber through a narrow gorge.
My fingers graze a granite face,
where millennia
the span of spider webs
have laid their green patina.

I've taken up a purpose to be small.
I've stripped myself
of summer's lush kiss of outdoor naps,
to labor among frozen bones of immutability.

I've taken up a purpose to be small.
Immersed, I halt my climb,
slow my breath,
stand motionless,
imperceptible.

THE FIRST DRAGONFLY

The first dragonfly along this Maine lake entices summer.
It hovers, pitches, yaws.
Crossing under shade, it flickers through each spot of sun.
On a stalk of phlox, it reflects iridescent blue,
a flake of mica, a mother-of-pearl chip hinging on transparent scissors.
Swept by breezes down the lake, swaths of tiger lilies bob,
a wave of Buddhist monks in prayer.
Facing gusts, oak leaf clusters hiss innocence.
An Adirondack chair offers up its single broken angle of repose.

But once, at each season's start,
a dragonfly explodes inside my eye as a Huey gunship
thumping down to momentary rest as jungle grass flattens away
in all directions, exposing us in crouching sprint
to and from its thinly armored doors.

Now, my joint grease hardening,
I cast a furtive backward glance onto a glint
issuing from the maw opening behind the self:
jaws of the bear that shakes off hibernation
to forage in the estuary of daydreams.
Alert and motionless, like on patrol,
I know that it will pass, its ursine grunt triggered
by a summer's agile dragonfly.

HER BLACK EYE

The plumbers entered the foyer, glanced,
but never said a word about it.
She greeted them with normal voice,
an ordinary tone of day,
a vague wave toward the guest bathroom.
They stood for a moment like men
outside a cave who have no light.
Their eyes flickered away from hers,
to here and there
like sparrows picking in a yard,
quickly, lightly.

Her left lower lid was swollen out
like a portion of plum, a dull gleam,
the lower edge draining into gravity
its blue, green, yellow
—an unreadable chromatograph.
The white of her eye was a moist flame,
a circle of red,
a living object trapped,
and looking out one of the keyholes of hell.

What is there about those initially relaxed encounters
when a stranger becomes captured
beneath a black curtain swallowing the air,
where a queasy balance falls on every word?
To that stranger, what could be poised among the rafters,
like a child's turquoise suitcase
with a Bakelite handle
swaddling an infant's bones long dried?
What tall mass could be throwing its shifting shadow
on the ceiling of the unused dining room?
Can any stranger question the interior dimensions
of another stranger's home?
Do all possessive men
misunderstand the limits of possession?

After their close confinement around a toilet,
bolted down and understood,
with caution, they offered up a bill.
Finally she laughed with curiosity.
"Would you have been so silent
if I'd had a broken leg?"

I Get Up Early

I get up early for the solitude. For then,
the earth slows down at one's command.
Black coffee is my frank companion,
and in the quiet, in the half-light,
the muse and I will hunt each other
playfully, sometimes earnestly, among the shadows.
Only the refrigerator hums.
Stalking is a silent game.
Unconscious, the others dream in flotsam fragments,
themselves adrift among the haloed streaks of dawn.
And about that muse?
Who's the feline, who the mouse?
And will I ever be released?
For like a beast, I want much sleep.

At Minimum, The Dusk

Clouds of infant pink
drift across
pale blue blanket
of sky,
a massive softness
silent
hardening to dark.

A black horizon
of trees stands
ragged like a burnt edge
of paper.

Eyes strain
into vacuity.
Salient features stand.
Submerging into dark
you might see
a dot of light or two
to organize
this disappeared landscape

A distant porch light steadfast
among a quavering of leaves.

A star with its narrative
mingled into night's
water-gray clouds.

A lone harbor light,
its reflection swimming in place
across a shifting tide,
a tide on which
to cut the day adrift.

Of a Fish Laid Onto a Dock

Disproportionate, the glass eyes
are fixed.
And what if
they could follow you
as you prepare to lift
the solemn texture of the flesh?

It flips against the boards,
rapid slapping dying down.
Nothing bleeds,
not slender articulations
that reciprocate white bone lips
torn
to free the barb.

Gills in garnet fronds fan out
beneath each scaly operculum
flexing open shut open shut:
the act of drowning.
Until you cup your hand prayer-like
behind its slippery head,
touch with your thin-honed knife
and push.

A Loon's Death

It starts with stabs,
black beak gaping scissors,
sudden, at the throat.
One young loon ascendant
descends full weight
onto a slowing one.

Along the lake, a territory lies
circumscribed in evergreens,
familial, thick with lurking food,
nesting spots.
The faltered loon
has betrayed its call with clues,
perhaps a sagging tremulo
along its lengthy soaring flute,
or a hitch half hidden
in its short and keening cry,
or in its garble warble:
a society of language
from the throats of all loons,
a tribe alert when eagles poach.

Wings, onyx heads,
torsos, webbed claw feet,
thrash the surface
as scree, scraw resound
to skim the hovering glass.
Violence pursues its single end.
Pairs of others
tuck around their young.

Once fixated by the neck,
the dying one gets dragged below,
a ragged silver trail of bubbles.
Fish will nip apart the sodden pulp.
Once again, a young loon
preens long dark blades
layered on his wings.

CADAVER

The gray cadavers stretched, looming though laid flat,
central to all other facts:
steel tables, a cold tiled room,
students standing in a clump.

We laid aside our stacks of scribbled notes,
to face up to a nude inside a plastic shroud.
I asked about the tag for mine—"A suicide at thirty-four."
The bag was damp inside.
An acrid breath of formalin arose.
I smoothed his matted hair,
touched his coldly muscled torso, eagle nose,
Roman lips incised into his face.

Across an outdoor table once
surely a woman measured him.
Smoothing her skirt,
she watched, alert to his square chest, soft hair,
as he probed his way through conversation
toward that fold between her breasts.
Overhead, sun-struck leaves allowed tatters of light
to swim on the white tablecloth.

My scalpel slits a bloodless seam across the chest
and I begin to peel up the greasy skin.
The muscles shine, strapped across the bones.
Deeper among membranes, does a clue exist
about his final sight—the self defiled?
Did his fingers swim before his eyes?
Did he inhale harder, sucking for carbon monoxide,
as pins of light began to swarm
inside the dark and running car?

Hunched at the stainless table, one foot up,
I laid aside the air drill,
chose a heavy blade to split the ribs,
jostling the eyeless skull.
Its sawed off cap lay facing up,
as if it were a shallow porcelain bowl,
white, undisturbed, filled with fragrant oil,
ready for prayers.

When I was done weeks on, there were only fat
and pieces of the spine.

OUR FEAR OF DOCTORS

Above the yawning incision,
two pairs of gloved and bloody hands
work smoothly like arms of the instinctual spider
weaving a geometry of stitches.
The surgeon's brain, however, shuffles and reshuffles,
directs the lacing, looking like railways on a map,
and hums an oratorio, with a pause to ask for clamps.
With skin, fat, fascia pulled back in layers
looking like a lurid smile,
the bulging organs, naked to the chilly air,
begin to gurgle and seep.
Eyes taped shut, the patient swims, yet cannot.

The gristly mass rests alone,
suffocating in a stainless pan.
The stout and lively floor nurse
takes sandwich orders from everyone.
Paralyzed, the patient hears the call for ham.

Somehow from my living room,
I have passed by screens with ghosts of my own bones,
and have arrived at a terminal place in the world,
mountains behind, with only sky and sea ahead,
shimmering, restful, implacable.
Bloated, I hobble on a precipice,
solitary, giddy, pawing my guts
back into my shirt so no one sees
while death works in my chest his endless filigrees.

But now, just now,
like floating backward, I am retrieved.
Far below, the gaunt
and pockmarked ferryman withdraws,
his knuckles white around the rigid oar.

I am just patient number three
in theatre number five.
My face emerges
through the brilliant surface.
My torso bucks.
Instinctively, I gasp the frigid air.

MEDICAL MISSION, GUATEMALA, 1997

I remember only three small circles,
the rest being chalk powder, falling away.
One rifle's muzzle tip, a hole into darkness,
inches from the car window, toward my face.
That, and two brown irises, impassive, meeting my raised glance.
Our driver wove a partial lie, the currency of roadblocks,
those transient clots of civil war, before the soldier waved us through.

Every rutted road we drove ended among Q'eqchi Mayans:
A coughing Rover spitting out boxes of amoxicillin,
scalpels, gauze, sutures, forceps, a generator.
Our hands searching into our only bucket of disinfectant,
opaque from blood. Gloved fingers creeping gingerly for rongeurs.
Excision of a small pumpkin's worth of orange worms.
A stillborn, distorted, color of clay.
Newborns, mewling in the fire of scabies, dysenteric, indigenous, dying.
Kwashiorkor, naked, sidling between two mud walls,
her teeth and pointed cheekbones turning to face me briefly,
before she levered her pendulous belly away, listless,
on spindles hung with skin.
Dust-crusted boys scampering in and out of the trash fire,
parading about in bloodied gloves, laughing like fiesta.
Oily smoke rolling over them.
The accusatory eyes of a young campesino,
machete dully gleaming in his belt.
The profuse jungle eating everything.
Sweating, we breathed through our masks,
an asthmatic straining for relevance.

And yet, for a single sunset,
with flocks of toucans skimming jungle canopy,
sweeping among the jutting heads of abandoned Mayan pyramids
we sat, spent, on a capstone, faces flushed with dying light.

THE UKRAINIAN PHARMACIST

I have dispensed it all.
Nursing at 3 AM to soothe our infant's cry.
Order in a prospering household? I dispensed that too.
Medications for the weak and ill? Yes, that was me at the window.
My quiver behind me, I am the archer
who, in aiming, plants my foot where I see fit.
I have fulfilled the faint oath drying to the lips
of every Tatiana, Vera, Yulia, Irena
who perished hiding in a ditch
as Russian tanks went grinding along the road.

I was reborn into a new fertile land.
My word, in Ihor's presence,
seals our marriage bond.
I have strode the length and breadth of life,
dispensing energy singing from my bones and muscles
until now when I feel bone begin to rub on bone,
until now when I feel small tears in my cartilage,
until now when, through a thousand titrations,
from a profusion of vials,
I have compounded knowledge into wisdom.

DISSECTION

The only path to medicine
goes through a cold and tiled dissection room.
All this to visualize a sunken elder,
or yet, a bald child laboring for breath,
as something like a gargoyle,
risen from a cocoon of wadded sheets,
opening up as if to fly, head brushing the ceiling,
draped arms spread,
fingers reaching forward with nails still growing.
When, after all, it's the human body dissected,
arteries and nerves like rubber strings,
muscles in their fatty wraps
fanned out like wings from every joint.
Leaning down to the cadaver,
the professor sets her hip against the curled lip of the steel table,
and tucked beneath her arm, her bone saw.
The student lingers back, as if he'd seen
an angel bristling with shards of glass,
who still might draw a breath,
lying in disarray among long tables of geraniums,
smelling of damp soil,
after crashing through the greenhouse ceiling.

First Appointment

Your false impressions? Pocket them.
Your brain, your body,
the contents of your torso's cavities have failed you.
Professional hands will intrude now.
Is it that rash? Could it be a lump?
Maybe it's your balance,
or that vague pain in your lower gut that wanders,
dragging your imagination by its thinning hair
back and forth at night
through a labyrinth of your very own design
cobbled together inside that cramped skull.
Did you earn that bleary face
ruminating in the mirror at odd hours?
This appointment could go to anywhere, from anywhere.
But it will pivot around that single moment when
someone will need to get so close
that you can identify deodorant and lunch.
Restrain yourself from that electric pulse of fear
when you might bolt off the table
scattering stainless steel canisters.
Or maybe you will encounter the one who,
in the subtle silent music of two hands, lost in focus,
brings off an intimacy
that is as effortless and complex as a skilled lover,
not of you but of the art.
You and every possibility will be elevated,
rotated through spatial planes,
back-lit, side by side,
with the progress of each intrusion.
Then both of you can start to heal.

The Ukrainian Festival

The old men sit to drink.
A shrinking lot these days,
they're careful not to numb with vodka
each man's lifelong sentry eye.
Heads will drift
to some reflective spot,
perhaps a knot in a picnic table top.
Their eyes lose focus,
hovering half a century and more
on a sunlit middle ground,
a field of wheat heavy in its August rhythm
a few meters short of hung menace in a tree line.

> I was a child.
> My brother was fourteen.
> Our Tato found him crumpled in the forest,
> wearing pieces of a uniform,
> not buried,
> partially consumed by wolves.
> German flamethrowers burned
> what the Russians
> didn't get the time to torch.

Unless you were there,
sometimes even if
you're born to blood,
every greeting gets
a terse reply,
every compliment
a shrug,
every handshake
a motionless grip.

Winslow Homer's Rendition

A line of boys with tension in their grips
uncoils from right to left in *Snap the Whip.*
They fly against full sun. Their bare feet skim
the meadow. Onto grass and trees, warmth pours,
diffuse and beckoning. Just barely seen,
appraising girls stand silent with a hoop.
In front, few scattered flowers lean for light.
And out of view, I sense a hum of bees,
a whitewashed box. The odor of red clover and
twined honeysuckle clings. Soft air hangs still.
The yelling boys hold tightly in this game
as one organic fluid flexing arc.
They're taut, controlled, yet free, lost in their play.
Steep mountains couch them, and the red plank school.
As if the sanctuary of this dream
belonged to us, our eyes relax and drift.

But do you see those dark trees hedging them?
Can you see that looming ridge where bright clouds
float beyond, unknowable, to where? Did
a family leave for Oregon? Are their
bleached bones lying loose, or in monuments?

In snap the whip, I've played the anchor, then
the middle, then the tumbling tail. I ran
within a string of rambling boys. Dried dirt,
fresh streaks of grass stains on my knees, each step
that proved a supple laxity, were my
rumpled composure as I headed home.

I took a bus out of my rural town,
and from our firing line in Khe Sanh's mud
we called in shells all night. I sweated hours
away, with thoughts of Matthew Brady's row
of Union dead, hands furled, with fly-blown eyes.
Now, when I visit home, I don't stay long.

The ridge stands over trees grown large or gone,
a few old friends, a bed, a red brick school.
A pebbled stream meanders, laced with sun.
Onrushing, arching trees along the road
out of town flicker light across my face.
Museum tickets for fine arts await.
Seen from my seventh story, buildings slice
late sun in angled blades that creep down gray
straight streets. Walls of Cubist glass panes glimmer
above. I've cut my life in parts, not halves,
not whole. I've filled my bed with precious stones:
stones nonetheless, the price of restlessness.

Once the Grunt Decides

Once the grunt decides,
he'll pitch the pigeon, twerp, caretaker
into his burlap bag, pull tight the mouth
throw it on his meaty back and go.
Once the grunt decides,
all words have flown like a mass of starlings
that bursts off a matchstick field
and flexing like a black accordion turns and disappears.
The grunt will crawl for years through tinder-dry grass
to find a sucked-in hole of ragged wire,
a puncture wound along the border fence.
Once the grunt decides,
his heart speckled from watching his brother slowly die,
he may bike for cancer coast-to-coast.
Once the grunt decides, he'll mangle his personal scaffold,
—like the one I built for mine—
linear and cool to the touch,
every knuckle bolted tight with rationales.
The grunt inhabiting my husk monopolizes my attention
when I can't sleep at night.
Once the grunt grinds his truck gears on the uphill,
it may be prayer from dawn to dusk the day before
the grunt decides.
Any grunt knows how to play long-held wrath,
like a child at a piano, attentively, one ember at a time.
Once the grunt decides, no polished priest,
no alcoholic confidante, can bear the weight.
No reasonable mate will stand astride the road.
Once the grunt decides,
he'll leave his cubicle neater than a pin
and when he gets to Uganda,
knee-deep in a cauldron of dirt, fly-specked,
he'll nurse his illness alone as he helps them sweep for mines,
some made to look like a piece of candy.

In rare extremes,
it's death, or suicide, or death accompanied by suicide
once the grunt decides.
You should lightly hold hands but do not stare.
In vacillation, grunts will sputter and flare
as though beneath a chemist's torch.
Moments before the burst,
they will ignore unintended consequence
that roils like smoke inside their darkening eyes.

SLEEP IN NAGASAKI

Sleep will not quietly draw a silk door
before my eyes tonight,
lying in this bed
in an inn in Nagasaki.
The mats are shaken out and clean.
The tea pot radiates heat into the table.
The silent maid brings water
and pads away.

There was not time enough
even to be startled.
A tired clerk rubbing his face,
an irritated girl calling in the garden
after her brother,
a small boy hiding
behind a twisted plum tree.
They became shadows of carbon
on stone walls.

There is a soft noise in the inn hallway.
Two voices murmur. There is a small giggle.
Two pairs of arms slide together.
From the garden outside,
a tree casts a deformed shadow
on the paper latticed door.
I have gathered the quilt around me.

> The falling bomb did not hesitate
> in passing through the veil of clouds.
> the instant came.
> massive waves of heat
> rolled outward in concentric spheres.
> quantum shells and neutrons alike dissolved.

Silk paintings of Buddha before his cave
were swallowed in the red air.

"What was this melting wind?
Even houses made of brick have vanished."

Unable to finish the evening paper,
Albert Einstein sits motionless at his desk until dawn.
Neils Bohr jerks bolt upright in his bed.
His wife assures him it is but a nightmare.

Taking Midwatch with C.S. Forester

I woke with a shudder, under groan of oak, pegged and lashed.
Turning out of my hammock, I knew these were
my buckle shoes from home,
but the orlop deck's velvet air belonged not to a brigantine,
nor a frigate,
but a man-of-war, block and tackle knocking in a luff, adrift,
and I was late for watch on helm.
The bell rang three.
Black archangels roiled beneath my feet.
I raced for the wheel deck, my mess-mate fast behind.
Halfway through the prisoners' passageway,
it collapsed from insubstantial arms grasping at me.
Had I not stowed their rations?
The gun-deck ceiling sagged in stifling heat,
and turning, I saw my mess-mate gone,
slumgullion thrown aside, an airy whistle left behind.
I burst on deck, saw clear constellations,
innumerable pinpricks of an overturned bowl
sealed dark around the horizon's rim,
a fury of light glowering beyond.
Shooting stars fell like claws above my head.
Craning up, I searched for any crew aloft.
Was that my bosun's form behind the topgallant sail,
or was it the mizzen mast wrapped by loose canvas?
Shivering, I feared that he would turn away
before he reached the spot
where we were supposed to meet.
The ship wallowed askew in greasy swells.
Sprinting up the ladder onto the quarterdeck,
my feet got tangled in abandoned clothing of the second mate.
A streak moistened the planks.
Was he dragged out on a path of stars,
or was that just the sheen of moon?
As I grabbed the unattended wheel, my breath pounded for dawn.
My eyes strained to make out
the profusion of masts, ropes, ladders, guns, decks.
Yet all were glimmers.
The bell rang two.

Seeing Blind at Navy Fire School

Gouts of smoke roll out,
a softened color,
like black mold thick on bread.
My head strapped tightly
inside my OBA,
any oxygen breathed in
smells like rubber sheened with oil.
Cumbered in a fire suit,
when will I wean myself
from jolting streaks of fear
that strip me of composure
as quickly as a fish's spine
gets zipped out on a cleaning table?

This morning
I was gotten up at reveille,
another donkey in the dark,
until I drew the short straw
to be first man of six
wrapped around a stiffening python
erupting water.

My rubber boots
slip and slubber forward
through hot bunker oil underfoot.
I'm foundering in smoke
until I force myself to lurch
the next five forward.
A slow forward,
through my blackening goggles.
A slow furious forward into dark.

When did I decide to pay attention?
When I remembered watching
through the jittery grain
the jumpy clip of film:
Their smoking ship in heavy list,
men dropping like families
into a sea on fire.

THE DECORATED MAN

Naked and exhausted
in the shipboard shower room,
we walked a widened berth
around the decorated man.
Mealy white, tall,
a burgeoning proportion like a grub,
he kept his distant look as he shaved,
a mess cook lost
among the sunburned deck apes.

His breasts bloomed
yellow chrysanthemums, Japanese in style.
Thin gold rings, round as suckle,
pierced his nipples.
Dragons, geishas, leopards, vines,
flocks of parrots, a pair of clawing cocks,
swirled up and down his limbs,
across his torso in a tidal flood:
the Peaceable Kingdom on opium sticks.

And all of it, forty years
before it swept the world.

Our First Class petty officer,
just his forearms slurred with tattoos,
rolled his eyes.
The cook did not respond.

Cook,
—without a name to us—
took the ladder
for any outbound Navy ship,
never going home.
Had he sought an Asian girl, a quiet one?
Yet, did she turn out to be the one
who'd hold his hand
fiercely walking through the marketplace?

Back home, years before,
in California, Florida, Minnesota,
did a crystal ball of American dream
within his reach explode,
and did a long curved shard
wound the cord of his every breath?
Did a cloud of flying slivers
speckle his every rationale?
Did he think tattoos were bandages
which never have to get removed?
Was this his shield of skin?

I watched him
in a steaming mirror of the shower room.
He would not return my gaze.
I examined his refraction stripe by colored stripe
through the accidental shards I possess.
Once learned,
I later forced myself to unlearn
the silence I laid on
to such a man.

A Dream of the T'ang Dynasty

You sat out on the riverbank all night
without a word.
I sat three paces back,
tending our covered lantern.
My listless brush balanced in my hand,
as I invented verse to pass the time,
inching through the inky hours.
A splash's sound rippled the air.
"A fish?" I offered. You did not respond.

That night your only remark was that
the black trees, vertical against the moon,
remind you of your wife,
when ropes of her wet hair hang
across her face,
as she rises from her bath.
Now, how many leagues away are we?

At your arrival,
your initial report had galloped off by courier,
a note short and sharp like a paring knife.
Your newly assigned frontier billows out
to bracken, mountain streams,
each gorge inhabited by honk of geese.
Their dark forms sweep low against the ridgeline
like marauders descending among star blue trees.

I've seen your wallet open to the poor,
not like most officials, pursing their lips.
I've seen you share wine with a stranger.
But you know when to stop.
Not us poets.

Ho Chih-chang, tumbling
in a stupor from his horse,
was discovered in a dry well,
curled up like Ying and Yang, snoring.
We know Li Po
was found face-down, afloat,
the moon inside his lungs.
You? You taste. You wait
for the wine to undress itself.
You reconstruct its rain, its clay and mineral,
its slopes of fields where millet sifts the sun,
the whole time wearing Buddha's face.

Now you must reconstruct defense
along this river valley floor,
an open throat to the interior.
Dawn breeze buffs a sea of millet grass
that undulates like battle banners.
Curt in your commands,
your ranks of stallions clatter
toward our kingdom's edge.

The fisherman and his wife once more
retreat into their hovel,
hiding under straw beneath a basket
their last curious boy.

By the next moon,
grass will drink
the wine that gurgles
out of warriors.

THE LOOMING 63

Our carrier captain ordered all hands down,
plowing toward a typhoon, off Hawaii, to the west.
A victory vee, the prow began to slash
a darkly speckled sea throwing back its combs.
Jet fighters delicate as scorpions
got dragged below and double-chained
like King Kong prior to the show.
Our flattop deck lay vacant, secured,
a void about to be awash.
Three thousand men, getting jostled at cards,
sat battened under decks.
But I, the scamp, the swabbie at nineteen
slipped out hyena-like,
out of modified general quarters
onto the lurching catwalk suspended off the edge.
To my right, the island jutted,
steel gray ascending into sky gray,
rolling seven decks aloft.
And across its flank, in overbearing white,
the block numbers 63,
the 63 that owned me
and my number too.
Whips of rain snapped at my dungarees,
and I listened for a siren in the storm
to learn if she would sing
my prankster name.

Right angled into blue-green troughs
the colossal mass wallowed
the way a downed battle horse
tries to rise from mud.
Shudders buckled my legs.
Swells the size of city blocks,
some peaking like a church, arose.

Curls of green walls collapsed
up on the flattop's leading edge.
A marl of clouds roiled, close enough,
it seemed, for me to rake my fingers through.

Weeks later, off the coast of Vietnam,
at night on deck I'd faintly hear
the siren, out among Pacific stars.
But towering in the dark, the 63.